S0-BIZ-347

The German Americans

PEG ASHBROCK

MAJOR AMERICAN IMMIGRATION

MASON CREST PUBLISHERS • PHILADELPHIA

A man dressed in traditional German clothing takes part in an Oktoberfest celebration. The celebration originated in Munich, Germany as a 16-day festival. Today, Germans around the world celebrate their heritage during October.

The German Americans

PEG ASHBROCK

MAJOR AMERICAN IMMIGRATION

MASON CREST PUBLISHERS • PHILADELPHIA

Mason Crest Publishers
370 Reed Road
Broomall PA 19008
www.masoncrest.com

Copyright © 2009 by Mason Crest Publishers. All rights reserved.
Printed and bound in Malaysia.

First printing

1 3 5 7 9 8 6 4 2

Library of Congress Cataloging-in-Publication Data

Ashbrock, Peg.
  The German Americans / Peg Ashbrock.
    p. cm. — (Major American immigration)
  Includes bibliographical references and index.
  ISBN-13: 978-1-4222-0607-2 (hardcover)
  ISBN-13: 978-1-4222-0674-4 (pbk.)
  ISBN-10: 1-4222-0607-6 (hardcover)
  ISBN-10: 1-4222-0674-2 (pbk.)
  1. German Americans—History—Juvenile literature. 2.
Immigrants—United States—History—Juvenile literature. I. Title.
  E184.G3A842 2008
  973'.0431—dc22
                                        2008026006

Table of Contents

MAJOR AMERICAN IMMIGRATION

America's Ethnic Heritage

Barry Moreno, librarian
Statue of Liberty/
Ellis Island National Monument

Ethnic diversity is one of the most striking characteristics of the American identity. In the United States the Bureau of the Census officially recognizes 122 different ethnic groups. North America's population had grown by leaps and bounds, starting with the American Indian tribes and nations—the continent's original people—and increasing with the arrival of the European colonial migrants who came to these shores during the 16th and 17th centuries. Since then, millions of immigrants have come to America from every corner of the world.

But the passage of generations and the great distance of America from the "Old World"—Europe, Africa, and Asia—has in some cases separated immigrant peoples from their roots. The struggle to succeed in America made it easy to forget past traditions. Further, the American spirit of freedom, individualism, and equality gave Americans a perspective quite different from the view of life shared by residents of the Old World.

Immigrants of the 19th and 20th centuries recognized this at once. Many tried to "Americanize" themselves by tossing away their peasant clothes and dressing American-style even before reaching their new homes in the cities or the countryside of America. It was not so easy to become part of America's culture, however. For many immigrants, learning English was quite a hurdle. In fact, most older immigrants clung to the old ways, preferring to speak their native languages and follow their familiar customs and traditions. This was easy to do when ethnic neighborhoods abounded in large North American cities like New York, Montreal, Philadelphia, Chicago, Toronto, Boston, Cleveland, St. Louis, New Orleans and San Francisco. In rural areas, farm families—many of them Scandinavian, German, or Czech—established their own tightly knit communities. Thus foreign languages and dialects, religious beliefs, Old World customs, and certain class distinctions flourished.

The most striking changes occurred among the children of immigrants, whose hopes and dreams were different from those of their parents. They began breaking away from the Old World customs, perhaps as a reaction to the embarrassment of being labeled "foreigner." They badly wanted to be Americans, and assimilated more easily than their parents and grandparents. They learned to speak English without a foreign accent, to dress and act like other Americans. The assimilation of the children of immigrants was encouraged by social contact—games, schools, jobs, and military service—which further broke down the barriers between immigrant groups and hastened the process of Americanization. Along the way, many family traditions were lost or abandoned.

Today, the pride that Americans have in their ethnic roots is one of the abiding strengths of both the United States and Canada. It shows that the theory which called America a "melting pot" of the world's people was never really true. The thought that a single "American" would emerge from the combination of these peoples has never happened, for Americans have grown more reluctant than ever before to forget the struggles of their ethnic forefathers. The growth of cultural studies and genealogical research indicates that Americans are anxious not to entirely lose this identity, whether it is English, French, Chinese, African, Mexican, or some other group. There is an interest in tracing back the family line as far as records or memory will take them. In a sense, this has made Americans a divided people; proud to be Americans, but proud also of their ethnic roots.

As a result, many Americans have welcomed a new identity, that of the hyphenated American. This unique description has grown in usage over the years and continues to grow as more Americans recognize the importance of family heritage. In the end, this is an appreciation of America's great cultural heritage and its richness of its variety.

The port city of Bremen sits on the Weser River in Germany. The oldest seaport in Germany, Bremen became a hub of commerce about 1,000 years ago.

1 The Trip of a Lifetime

Elisabeth Knapke's dream was like many others in the early 19th century. She dreamed of free land, religious freedom, and a better life. By the 1800s, many *emigrants* began to seek relief from the poverty, famine, and overpopulation of Germany by traveling to United States or Canada.

After months of consideration, the decision was made. Elisabeth was going to leave everything she knew and loved. The sacrifice was great, but the dreams of the New World lured her. The chance to make a new start, to settle in an uncharted country was a dream so powerful that she would leave her home, her family, and her friends to build a new life far away in a developing land. It was the trip of a lifetime.

Elisabeth was an unusual young woman. She decided to leave her country and travel across the ocean with friends from her small village. Although Elisabeth's family was not well-off, she was fairly well-educated. She knew how to read and write. Elisabeth kept a detailed diary of her daily life and her journey to the New World.

It was "a bleak and miserable day" on the first day of Elisabeth's journey to America, and she suffered strong feelings about her decision to emigrate. She was coming to marry Bernard Boeke, a childhood friend who had immigrated to Cincinnati, Ohio, the year before.

Elisabeth's journey began in her hometown in northern Germany. She was traveling with friends to the German port city of Bremen. For eight long days, they alternated walking and riding in a wagon, starting early each day, taking only bread and eggs with them for that day's journey. The days passed slowly. "We learn again it takes time and patience" Elisabeth wrote. "This is just the beginning, and we know nothing."

Once they arrived in Bremen, Elisabeth and her fellow travelers spent the next 15 days talking with the representatives of various ships. After considering the costs and the *accommodations*, Elisabeth decided to take a sailing ship to Baltimore, Maryland, and then finish her journey by wagon to Cincinnati.

She purchased a bed in a cabin that was the size of a sleeping alcove in her home and came with two drawers under the *berth* for storage. That was all the room she was allowed for her living articles for the nearly 60-day journey to America. Nor was she alone; she shared her room with seven other people.

Before boarding the ship, Elisabeth spent time talking with others in the port who knew something about the journey. She learned about safety, what daily life was like on the ship, and what she needed to pack for her voyage. Passengers were responsible for their own food, cooking, and serving utensils. They also had to bring all the goods they would need for their new life in America.

Elisabeth and others boarded the ship and spent the night before departure on board. Early the next morning, the captain steered the ship up the Weser River towards the North Sea. It took three days for the ship to travel along the Weser and enter the North Sea. The ship then had to pass through the North Sea, traveling along the European coastline before crossing the Atlantic Ocean. The captain tolled the bell as the ship began this extraordinary voyage at sunrise.

Elisabeth kept a daily log of her long and often dangerous journey, beginning with Day One in the North Sea. "The

A German liner, the *Europa*, arrives at port on her maiden voyage to New York from Bremen, Germany. Like other immigrants, many Germans spent much of their savings to pay for the cramped ocean voyage, with the hope of starting a new life in America.

wind is powerful and strong. The ship trembles and rocks and twists from side to side, and then come great waves, end to end, and my stomach feels sick again. I have not eaten; I was so sick, as were all the other travelers."

Elisabeth and her fellow travelers were frequently seasick. Most immigrants of the early 19th century came to America on heavily packed wooden ships that pitched and rolled in the high seas. There was a constant danger of the ship being destroyed by the rough waves.

A man wears a traditional Transylvanian costume at the Oktoberfest in Munich, Germany. The style of his costume originated in the 15th century and was in daily use until the end of the 19th century.

During fierce storms the sailors who took their turns at watch were tied to the mast with ropes so they would not be lost at sea.

Safety was also the focus of the passengers. Threat of fire from candles or open cooking fires was constant. Disease could and did spread rapidly in these tight quarters, and there was little or no medical care. Some died during the voyage. The bodies were sewn into an old piece of canvas with a stone at the foot. All the passengers would assemble on deck, pray, and sing hymns until the body was lowered into the ocean.

Elisabeth's trip was eventful. "We must endure the shaking and the noise mid-decks, the children crying," her diary reports. "People are very much afraid, and alone. We cooked once in our iron pot. It is not cool here between the ceiling and our floor; the smells, the sweat, the smoke, and the many dirty people are revolting. The stench is dreadful, but the commotion more so."

The travelers encountered frequent storms. "Our ship was thrown sideways and back and forth at the same time," Elisabeth wrote. "The wind and constant motion, the uncertainty and fear, are continual." During the storms, cooking was not allowed—sometimes for days. Passengers and sailors then existed on **hardtack** and stale water.

Other days it was still. There was no wind, so the ship was motionless. This could also last for days at a time. During those long days of inactivity, the passengers' thoughts turned from their journey to their future. "We thought about our new fatherland, and discovered in our minds a counterstream of thoughts about our abandoned homeland," Elisabeth wrote in her journal. "The trip is costly not merely in money, but also in these contrary feelings."

The passengers traveled alone or in family groups, yet mingled with unfamiliar people of every class. There were no class divisions or social ranks on board, other than the size of the cabin purchased for the voyage. Those with the most money purchased larger, more spacious cabins and were able to establish some privacy. Most travelers weren't that fortunate. They were packed together in tight, cramped quarters, and only occasionally were they allowed to go on deck during calm days.

Elisabeth's journey was a long one. It was 54 days before she saw the distant outlines of land for the first time, according to her journal entries. "This morning we saw land for the first time, thank God. Around 12 o'clock a pilot ship came and took us in escort to Baltimore, and in an hour we saw the long-craved-for land. Our goal is now here."

After fighting strong headwinds, the ship finally moved up the channel toward the shallower water and the entrance to the port. The anchor was dropped, and the police and a doctor came on to visit. "Not a single person on our ship was sick, and no one had died during our voyage," Elisabeth wrote. Her experience was not typical.

American inspectors boarded all arriving ships and checked the passengers. The rich, as well as the obviously ill, could leave when the ship docked. The poor had to take ferryboats to the inspection station to be examined. The United States didn't accept people with serious health problems; they were sent back to their old homes. Many immigrants didn't speak English and didn't understand what was happening.

With chalk, doctors wrote letters on the clothes of anyone who seemed sick. They paid extra attention to the marked people. Children with common diseases like measles were sent to the hospital. At every station, immigrants dreaded the eye exam. Doctors looked for *trachoma*, an eye disease that caused blindness.

The immigrants had to answer questions, as the government had just recently begun to keep statistics on immigration. They were asked where they were from and how much money they had. Officials wrote

PACKING LIST FOR AMERICA

Few lists of the items that immigrants brought with them to America exist today, but in her diary, Elisabeth Knapke included the list that both she and Bernard brought, as well as their seed list to start their American farm.

In addition to what he was wearing, Bernard's list included: shirt, pants, suspenders, nightshirt, wool coat, gloves, snow boots, handkerchief, chewing tobacco, iron needle, crucifix, prayer book, bottle of holy water, baptismal certificate and other personal papers, soap, cream, drinking cup. In his trunk he packed books, bed linen, lamp, sealing wax and seal, pliers, mallet, scissors, twine, tacks, spoon, knife, kettle, plate, pillows, leather apron, and medicine. On Bernard's food list he packed sugar, flour, salt, bacon, bread, rice, beans, potatoes, lard, sauerkraut, honey, and chocolate wafers.

In addition to what she was wearing, Elisabeth's lists included: long underwear, woolen petticoat, apron, nightgown, dress, coat, gloves, handkerchief, snow boots, candles, drinking cup, baptismal certificate and personal papers. In her trunk, she packed books, mirror, bed linen, paper, ink in bottle with stopper, pillows, blankets, purse, thimble, buttons, cotton thread, silk thread, yarn, needles, plates, knife, spoons, forks, and towels. She packed her foodstuffs as well: sugar, flour, salt, bacon, meat, bread, dried apples, rice, beans, potatoes, and sauerkraut.

To start their farm, Elisabeth and Bernard brought vegetable seeds: turnips, onions, cabbage, spinach, beets, parsnip, and carrots. Fruits included gooseberry, blackberry, strawberry, apples, cherries, peaches, pears, and apricots. They brought seed corn, oats, wheat, clover, barley, rye, and flowers, especially Elisabeth's favorites: margarita, snapdragon, peonies, lady slipper, morning glory, tulip, and crocus.

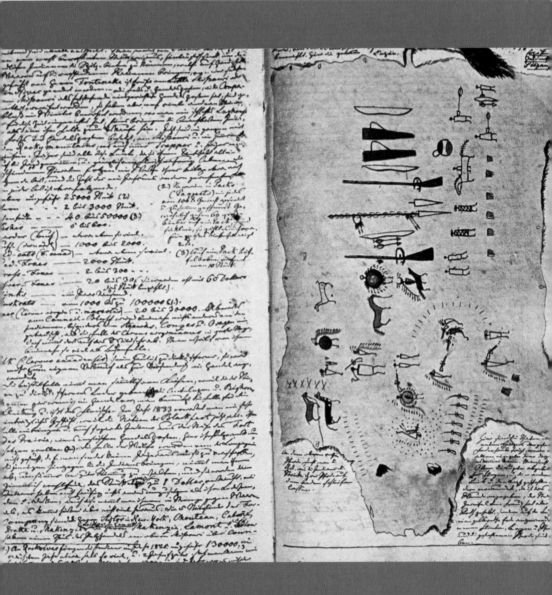

These two pages are from the journal of German traveller Prince Maximilian Alexander Philipp von Wied-Neuwield, who explored North America accompanied by artist Karl Bodmer. The page on the right depicts an example of Native American art as painted onto an animal skin.

notes about their hometowns, families, and jobs.

The United States wanted people who could take care of themselves. Helpers translated the many questions and answers. Within a day, most people received a landing card that allowed them to leave.

Immigrants who failed inspection had to stay in the ports at the immigration centers until a ship took them back overseas. Women and children who passed inspection were not allowed to leave until a man from the family met them or sent a letter or a ticket for them. They waited days, weeks, and even months before they were allowed to leave.

Elisabeth's experience was different. She had money, a destination, and someone to meet her. "This trip is a powerful, profound experience for me. The first impression as I saw America: It is a joyful sight and a lovely land."

Elisabeth's trunks were unloaded from the ship and brought up on shore. "My heart rejoiced. It is now time to resume my journey to meet Bernard in Ohio." ✷

This is the view from Heidelberg Castle, which overlooks a scenic city in the Rhine River Valley that dates back to Medieval times. The modern state of Germany did not exist before the 1870s; until that time, the region was a collection of small states, ruled from castles like Heidelberg by noble families.

2 Leaving Home

From the earliest days of this country, people born elsewhere came to America searching for a better life. Some were fleeing *persecution* and political turmoil. Many came for economic reasons. Others came for the chance to start a new life unencumbered by old traditions.

Their experiences were as diverse as their cultures, and so were their dreams. Some became farmers. Others toiled in factories. Still others brought their talents as builders, businessmen, and artists. By settling new regions and cities, providing a constant source of inexpensive labor, and by bringing their unique forms of political and cultural history, together they contributed to the building of a nation.

Before the founding of the German Empire in 1871, no single country called "Germany" existed. Germanic Europe was a network of tiny states. The people we call Germans were tied not by where they lived, but by their common language, culture, customs, and heritage.

About 2,000 years ago, the Germanic peoples had started spreading over much of Europe. In later centuries, whole groups would uproot themselves from one place in Europe and move to another. The migration to America was part of this wandering pattern.

The first German to reach the New World may have been a sailor named Tyrker, who sailed on a voyage with Scandinavian sea explorer Leif Ericson. Sometime around the year A.D. 1000, Ericson landed on

Labrador, an island off the coast of Canada. However, the large waves
of immigrants to North America would begin much later in history.

During the 16th and 17th centuries, Europe was involved in a series
of bloody wars over religion, politics, and money. The region that today
is called Germany was then made up of more than 200 different states.
The people of the different states followed different religions, so wars
soon erupted. Because of the tangle of political alliances that existed
throughout Europe, this became an international war. Three decades of
fighting, known as the Thirty Years War (1618–1648), fueled Germans'
desire to move to a country free from constant warfare.

In the early 1680s, an Englishman named William Penn visited the
German states, encouraging Germans to emigrate to a new colony he had

This map from the 1760s shows the many small states that existed in the region known as Germany. Wars for control over the region led many people to leave Germany and travel to the New World.

A Medieval castle overlooks a vineyard in the Rhineland region of Germany. This lush agricultural area was devaststed during the Thirty Years War. Many Germans living in the Rhineland decided to leave for America.

founded in America. Penn offered the Germans religious freedom and farmland. On October 6, 1683, 13 families from the town of Krefeld came to Pennsylvania. These first German Americans established a community called Germantown, which still exists as a neighborhood of Philadelphia.

Over the next century, periodic wars and crop failures would lead many other Germans to journey to America. Farmers, laborers, servants, and *artisans* were the most likely to leave Germany. These people dreamed of starting a new life in America.

William Penn was an English Quaker who traveled to the New World and established the colony of Pennsylvania in the late 17th century. Many Germans soon flocked to the colony. These farmers became known as Pennsylvania Dutch (from *Deutsch*, the German word they used to describe themselves). Their influence is still felt in the central part of the state, particularly around Lancaster and Lebanon.

Two factors often caused families to leave their home: push factors and pull factors. A push factor pushes you away from your old country. These may be economic problems such as crop failures, low wages, underemployment, and so on. A pull factor entices you to a new country. These were found in America: cheap land, industrial progress, high wages, and the chance to move up in society.

Many more German *peasants* followed during the 18th century. The agents of shipping companies and recruiters for the American colonies made extensive efforts to attract immigrants. They traveled through the Rhineland in brightly colored wagons. Those who had no money for their trip arrived in America as "redemptioners," or *indentured servants*. They agreed to work for a period of four to seven years to pay off the cost of their ship's passage. American colonial landowners came aboard the newly arrived ships to buy redemptioners in a system that was like temporary slavery.

By the 1750s, Germans were living in each of the 13 colonies. However, most Germans lived in the colonies of New York, New Jersey,

GERMAN-AMERICAN DAY

In 1983, President Ronald Reagan officially declared October 6 as German-American Day. This date was chosen to celebrate 300 years of German presence in America, honoring the contributions of German immigrants to the life and culture of the United States. It is a time of celebration, of raising awareness, strengthening a sense of identity, and pride in the contributions of German-speaking immigrants and their descendants to the building of this nation. The designation "German" is used in a cultural, not political, sense to include the German-speaking Swiss, Alsatians, Austrians, Germans from Eastern Europe, and German Jews.

In 1995, the United German-American Committee of the United States passed a resolution to "declare the period from mid-September to mid-October German-American Heritage Month." Most large celebrations and activities in the German-American community, such as Oktoberfests, concerts, exhibits, and other special events, frequently occur during this time.

and Pennsylvania. Few settled in southern colonies, such as Maryland, Virginia, the Carolinas, and Georgia, because many were opposed to slavery on religious grounds. They also stayed away from the south because a free laborer could not compete with the slave economy.

The pace of German emigration slowed from 1790 to 1815, in part because of the Napoleonic Wars that engulfed all of Europe. They became years of *assimilation* rather than expansion for the German-American population. After Napoleon's defeat, Germans in rural areas again began to seek relief from poverty, famine, and overpopulation by emigrating.

Until about 1830, most emigrants sailed from the Dutch port of Rotterdam or the French city of Le Havre. Later, the German port of Bremen became the main departure point. Bremen was referred to as "the suburb of New York" by the mid-19th century.

A few decades later, Hamburg attracted emigrants from eastern and southern Germany. During the 20th century, Hamburg became the chief port of emigration as large passenger-carrying steamships established regular routes across the Atlantic.

During the 19th century, religious persecution played a role in the push to emigrate. Passage of *anti-Semitic* laws in Bavaria and other German states from the 1830s to the 1880s forced many German Jews to leave their homes and seek a better life elsewhere.

A failed revolution in 1848 brought several thousand Germans to America. Known as the "forty-eighters," these liberal, *agnostic* intellectuals were to have a tremendous effect on German-American

A modern view of Hamburg, which today is the second-largest city in Germany. By the early 20th century, Hamburg was a major point of departure for German immigrants headed to America.

life. Many had edited or written newspapers in Germany, and became involved in journalism when they reached America. Most regarded the press as a vehicle for social change. Many worked to unite different groups around issues that affected all Germans in the New World.

A major wave of emigration hit the northern German states of Westphalia and Hanover in the 1850s. It peaked in 1854, when 215,000 people left their homelands. Nearly 1.3 million Germans left in that decade alone, including many highly skilled, well-educated professionals, such as doctors, lawyers, teachers, scientists, and industrialists. A second wave of German immigrants arrived in America during the 1860s, and within 10 years, another one million had come to America. Another heavy migration of Germans occurred from 1880 to 1893 when approximately 1.8 million made their way to the New World. Many left their homelands to attacks because of their *ethnicity*, religion, or politics.

Upheaval in Germany caused much of the mass emigration. In 1862, Otto von Bismark became prime minister of Prussia. He was determined to unite the German lands under Prussia's leadership by forging a military alliance of German states. The Franco-Prussian War ended in 1870 with all the German states united into one German empire. Bismark standardized all the legal, financial, and governmental systems and launched a *Kulturkampf* (culture struggle) to reduce the influence of the Roman Catholic Church in Germany. German Catholics responded by emigrating to North America, where they settled in cities like Milwaukee, Cincinnati, St. Louis, and

Alberta, Canada. Some of the German newcomers ended up settling in Canada's western provinces.

Immigrant numbers to the U.S. slowed during the war years of the American Civil War (1861–65), the Franco-Prussian War in Europe (1870–71), and especially World War I (1914–18). In between, however, huge numbers of Germans came to America.

A statue of Otto von Bismarck in a Berlin park. The "iron chancellor" helped turn Germany from a weak confederation of small states into a powerful empire during the second half of the 19th century.

When the United States entered the First World War against Germany and its allies, many Americans attempted to distance themselves from German culture. The derogatory term "Hun" was used to refer to Germans. Many German-language newspapers were closed down, and German foods were removed from menus or renamed.

From 1923 to 1963, the number of German arrivals on the shores of the United States still outnumbered those from any other country. During the 1930s, many were Jews seeking refuge from Hitler's anti-Semitic policies.

After 1945, another wave of German emigrants flooded the U.S. to escape the devastation caused by World War II. The post-war division of Germany into East and West Germany brought about a half million additional refugees, most fleeing Communist East Germany.

Because they arrived at different periods and at a variety of ports, German immigrants settled all over Canada and the United States. Many stayed in the cities with strong German cultures: St. Louis, Cincinnati, Milwaukee, Philadelphia, and parts of the Middle Atlantic states and the upper Midwest. In Canada, they concentrated near Toronto and in Nova Scotia, British Columbia, and Saskatchewan.

In the three centuries since the first German-American settlement was founded, about 7 million German-speaking emigrants have made their way to North America. They and their descendants form the largest single ethnic group in the U.S. today. ✹

Many of the German immigrants during the 18th and 19th centuries had been farmers in their native homelands. These immigrants settled in agricultural areas, where they acquired land and started small family farms like this one in Lancaster, Pennsylvania.

3 Immigrants Find a Home

They came looking for a better life. From small towns and villages to the large, bustling, cultural cities of Germany, they traveled here to a changing America that was both parts frontier and urban center. These newcomers settled all over the United States and Canada, often deciding to live near others who shared their same hopes and dreams, spoke their language, and practiced a familiar religion.

Early in the 18th century, many German immigrants went to Philadelphia. In 1709, the government of England encouraged several hundred Germans to go to New York by giving them land north of the city in return for their labor. A decade later, the French government attempted to colonize the territory of Louisiana by inviting German settlers to New Orleans. For the rest of the 18th century, German immigrants stepped off ships to begin their lives in virtually all the colonial ports, from Boston to Baltimore, Charleston to Savannah.

The majority of the Germans arriving during colonial times were farmers. They moved further into Pennsylvania, up the Hudson River in New York, and into northern New Jersey. A few went to New England, and settled in the Broad Bay region and along the Kennebec River in what later became Maine. German colonial farmers also settled in Virginia, Maryland, Delaware, the Carolinas, and Georgia.

Before the Civil War, two of the major U.S. exports to Europe were cotton and tobacco. Cotton was shipped from New Orleans to the port of Le Havre, France, and tobacco frequently went from Baltimore to Bremenhaven in northern Germany. To avoid coming back with empty ships, the captains of these vessels took emigrant passengers, most of whom were German, back to the United States. Sizable numbers of these new immigrants moved up the Mississippi River from New Orleans or inland on the Baltimore and Ohio Railroad.

In 1843, the independent Republic of Texas invited a group of **Hessians** to settle in Texas. The next year, about 150 families arrived in Brownsville, a port on the Gulf of Mexico. They founded the city of New Braunfels, which later became the gateway for many other German settlers. Texas became part of the United States in 1845.

From 1846 to 1915, many Europeans entered the U.S. at Galveston, Texas. Promoted by Rabbi Henry Cohen and the large Jewish-American community, Galveston called itself the gateway to the Midwest. It proved second to New York in its ability to attract immigrants. Thousands of Germans also took the long sea journey around the southern tip of South America to reach San Francisco during the Gold Rush of 1849 over the next few years.

Expansion continued westward with the passage of the Homestead Act in 1862. German immigrants brought with them a hardy red winter wheat that could be planted in the fall and survive the harsh winters of the northern plains states. The newcomers grew this wheat in the Dakotas, Nebraska, Kansas, and parts of

An immigrant leaves the Ellis Island ferry, carrying her possessions on her back and in her arms. The papers in her hand are probably instructions of where to go or the names of relatives already living in the United States.

Colorado, helping to turn the vast grasslands into wheat fields that would become the breadbasket of America.

German-speaking immigrants from the Russian Empire also put down roots in California, planting the grapevines that now flourish as world-renowned vineyards. Settlers from the Volga region centered on

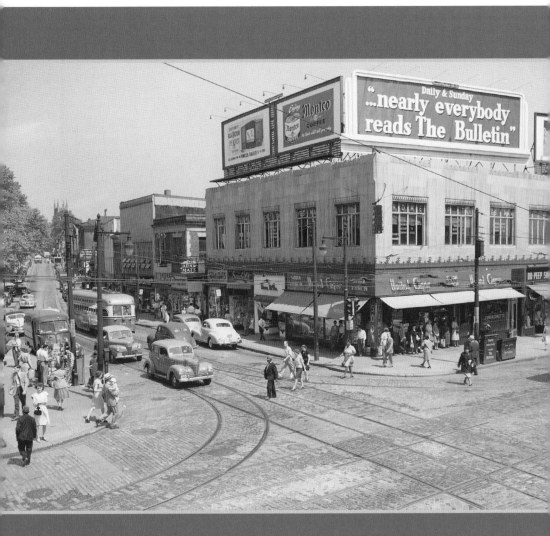

In 1683, German immigrants under the leadership of
Francis Daniel Pastorius founded the neighborhood
of Germantown in Philadelphia. Germantown was
home to one of the largest colonial printing presses,
and was also the summer home of President George
Washington in 1793 and 1794.

Lodi in central California. Black Sea Germans formed communities around Fresno, where they helped establish a raisin industry.

The largest number of German Americans took up dairy farming. The dairy belt included parts of upstate New York, Wisconsin, Michigan, and Minnesota. German dairy farmers often lived near large cities, so their cheese, butter, and milk could be delivered to urban markets.

In the early 19th century, most of the German immigrants were young, unmarried males. Later in the century, entire families made the journey together.

Well-educated Germans, some of whom had attended universities, fled during various periods—1819, the 1830s, and the late 1840s—when the German state governments sought to repress liberal movements that attracted students, teachers, and intellectuals.

The wave of German immigration to Canada saw large settlements in Ontario; the Maritime provinces, especially Halifax, and the Annapolis Valley in Nova Scotia; along the St. Lawrence River; in Quebec; and in Toronto. Western Canada's German settlement occurred in the late 19th century with miners following the gold rush to settle in Alberta and Saskatchewan.

The process of emigration could be difficult. The German states required all family members to obtain emigration *visas*. Emigrants had to provide such documents as baptismal and marriage certificates from their local church, evidence of having a trade or profession, and proof that adult males had fulfilled their military service. Charitable organizations, in cooperation with governmental agencies, sometimes supplied emigrants with a travel guide, a map of the railroad lines in the U.S., and a list of German settlements where they would be welcome.

New York was the nation's principal port of entry for German immigrants. Some of Germany's charitable organizations established offices in New York to help newcomers. Baltimore was the second most-common port of arrival for German immigrants in the late 19th century. Other frequent ports of entry for Germans were the cities of Boston, Galveston, Mobile, New Orleans, Philadelphia, San Francisco, and Seattle.

It was common for German immigrants and German Americans to move west with the frontier during the 19th century. German Americans contributed to the growth of such important midwestern cities as Chicago (opposite, top) and St. Louis (bottom).

The German-American conflicts of World War I and World War II dramatically decreased German immigration as anti-German hysteria spread through the United States. Emigration hinged on the political climate in both these areas.

Immigration from Germany fell after World War II. By 1972, many calling themselves German were third-generation German Americans. ✳

A young woman works at a cigar factory in Pittsburgh, Pennsylvania. Manual labor was usually the only option available to immigrants, who often had little money and few connections to secure a good job.

4 Life in America

Fitting in or making do was the watchword for immigrants; they had to learn to change to fit the American way of life. German immigrants, however, would not give up their culture. Along with all the things necessary for their physical existence, they placed an emphasis on their cultural heritage, their language, their way of life, their personal concepts, their value systems, their plans for the future, and their hopes and expectations.

The German immigrants were a practical people. They arrived in America hoping to earn a good living as tradesmen, artisans, or farmers. Many came with their entire life savings, which often was enough to start a small business or purchase land for a farm. They chose their sites carefully. Businessmen looked for a good location in a neighborhood that needed their services, while farmers often chose land near forests that could supply timber for fuel and building.

People fresh off the boat were called "greenhorns." Farmers didn't stay long in their port cities. They set off as quickly as possible to stake a claim on land and then to start their new lives.

Those who stayed in the city were crowded into tiny apartments in tall buildings. Families often slept, cooked, and ate in one room. Their homes lacked clean air and light, and often also became their workplace. Many of the new arrivals could not speak English. Until they learned the language, German immigrants had to take whatever work they could find. Whole families worked long hours for low pay.

In most families, everyone worked. Women and children rolled cigars, hemmed sleeves, or made brooms at home. They were paid by the piece. Some girls took jobs as servants. Men worked in factories or as laborers. Boys worked for their keep in *sweatshops*. They shined shoes, sold newspapers, collected rags, delivered messages, or peddled peanuts.

However, German Americans were more likely than members of other immigrant groups to find jobs as skilled workers. Most Germans had learned trades in their native land as bakers, butchers, brewers, tailors, barbers, carpenters, cabinetmakers, and gardeners, so they did not have to start at the bottom as low-paid, unskilled laborers. Some workers who had served as redemptioners to pay their passage to America had learned trades as *apprentices*.

SCHOOL DAYS

During the 19th century, when children could be excused from their chores, they often attended school in crude, one-room cabins. Wooden benches lined the walls, serving as both desks and chairs. A smoky stove centered in the room was their only heat; their lighting came from oil lamps hung from the rafters. School days were long, and all the students studied together in one large class. Those who did go to school often sat next to children from many different countries in class. In school these students were taught to love their new country. They saluted the flag and played American games like baseball.

Some immigrants demanded better wages and working conditions. They formed labor unions and organized marches and strikes. Bakers, tailors, and cigar makers formed local trade unions in New York, Philadelphia, Milwaukee, St. Louis, and Chicago. In the 20th century, the growth of assembly-line industries created a new wave of labor organizing. Walter Reuther, a German American, became active in the struggle to organize automobile workers during the 1930s. He served as president of the

A boy whistles as he shines shoes to make extra money for his family. Young immigrants worked nearly as often as older ones, since families needed all the money they could earn.

During World War II—a war in which the United States joined with other nations to fight against Nazi Germany—Dwight D. Eisenhower served as commander of the allied forces. Eisenhower, whose family was German American, was later elected president of the United States, serving from 1952 to 1960.

United Auto Workers (UAW) from 1946 until his death in 1970.

German Americans dominated the printing industry, both as laborers and as journalists. As architects, German Americans played a significant role in the architecture of American cities during the 19th century. Where Germans settled, their style of design can still be seen in buildings today.

German immigrant craftsmen who settled in Pennsylvania brought with them styles of peasant folk art from southwest Germany. These folk craftsmen often painted their furniture, decorating it with colorful designs of tulips and other items. This style of painting is now called

Pennsylvania German folk art. During the second half of the 19th century, large numbers of German cabinetmakers came to America to escape the restrictions imposed upon them by the European *guild* system. One result of this was the concentration of large numbers of skilled cabinetmakers in such American cities as Philadelphia, New York, and Cincinnati.

German merchants also opened taverns stocked with beer. In the early 1700s, breweries were established in New York, Baltimore, Milwaukee, Cincinnati, and in St. Louis. By the end of the 19th century, there were hundreds, each with its own formula for making beer. The passage of the 18th Amendment in 1919, which made alcoholic beverages illegal, wiped out many of the smaller breweries.

The German immigrants dominated the industries of bookbindery and papermaking. They were carpenters, blacksmiths, and tailors in New York and Chicago; *cobblers* in the mid-Atlantic; ironworkers in the eastern states; stonemasons in the south; and they ruled the stockyards in Chicago and Cincinnati.

The relatively high-paying jobs enabled the wives of these German newcomers to remain at home in a traditional role. Relatively few German women entered the labor force except as teachers or domestic servants.

Many immigrants who arrived in the early 19th century were university graduates. They found jobs as teachers, journalists, and clerks. In 1914, Cincinnati had four daily German newspapers, four hospitals staffed entirely by German-speaking doctors and nurses, and more than 70 churches where the services were in German.

These newcomers started schools to preserve their culture and to keep their languages and religions alive. By law, children were supposed to go to school until they were 16. But many businesses posted "Boy Wanted" signs, and children often went to work because most families needed the money. Often, only the youngest children studied full time.

Schools held evening classes to help parents learn the language and customs of their new country. Older immigrants offered loans and advice to new arrivals. Rich Americans also felt a duty to help the immigrants. They opened settlement houses to help newcomers learn American ways. Part school and part neighborhood center, a settlement house usually had a playground, a library, a gym, and a kitchen. Volunteers gave classes in how to wash, dress, and cook American-style.

Within tightly knit communities, supporting family and adhering to culture was a strong bond. Preservation of traditional German dress, language, and entertainment was important even while adapting to their new country's own styles. Today, the Bavarian *dirndl* for girls and the white shirt and *lederhosen* for the boys are the traditional items of clothings most associated with the German immigrants.

They founded clubs like the Order of the Sons of Hermann to foster German customs and language to help financially needy members. Many other clubs, including social clubs, were formed in large communities. Some were associations of people from the same state in Germany; others were for specific purposes, such as the gymnastics clubs.

Hex signs—the round, multicolored decorations that incorporate star-like patterns, such as the ones on the wall of this barn—are a common sight in central Pennsylvania. The signs are a form of folk art practiced by the Pennsylvania Germans who came to America before 1800.

Equally popular were German singing societies. Choral singing was a beloved tradition. Sangerfests (singing festivals) featured a mix of German folk songs and classical music. Wherever Germans settled in America during the 19th century, they established choral groups and musical societies. Today, popular German cultural festivals—the Oktoberfests, Germanfests, and Strassenfest—are celebrated in cities all over America.

German-born John A. Roebling (inset) perfected the techniques of building suspension bridges. His greatest achievement was his design of the Brooklyn Bridge in New York.

5 German-American Culture Today

German Americans brought to the New World all the cultural variety of their homeland. They touched America not only as individuals, but also as a group. They brought customs that are now considered part of the American way of life, such as food, culture, and even cherished holiday traditions. Today, 49 million Americans can claim partial or full German ancestry, making them the country's largest ethnic group. The real story of the German Americans is not so much what they have achieved for themselves, but what they have contributed to the development of the United States and Canada as it is today in industry, science, culture, military strength, and recreation.

Immigrants made lasting contributions to their new land. For example, German-trained Jewish rabbis, such as Isaac M. Wise from Bohemia, introduced the idea of reformed Judaism in the United States. After 1830, Jews from Germany began forming their own *congregations*.

Immigrants had an enormous influence on U.S. agriculture. German farmers are credited with introducing the crop rotation system known as diversified farming, and for using barnyard manure, red clover, and gypsum for fertilizers. Pioneers explored the frontier with a Kentucky rifle developed and perfected by immigrant German craftsmen. Families traveled across the prairie states in a Conestoga wagon that German wagonmakers had designed and named for a creek near Germantown, Pennsylvania. Many immigrants were experts in such areas as carpentry, weaving, and **masonry**. Their places of work were workshops, not merely stores. German Americans have more than touched America's industrialization.

It's hard to name an industry that is not associated with German immigrants. From iron and steel to pianos and chocolate bars, all were German companies that started with an idea. German Americans founded major American businesses such as HJ Heinz, Mueller's, Folgers, Levi Strauss and Co., Bausch and Lomb, and Westinghouse. John Roebling came to America and began building bridges in the mid-19th century across Niagara Falls, the Ohio River in Cincinnati, and his most famous work, the Brooklyn Bridge. His major innovation was the

Carl Schurz was born in Germany, and was involved in the failed revolution of 1848. After this, he left Europe for America, arriving in 1852. Schurz served as a Union Army commander during the Civil War, and in 1869 became the first German American elected to the U.S. Senate.

Thomas Nast became a political cartoonist for *Harper's Weekly* in 1862 and created such famous American symbols as the Republican elephant and the Democratic donkey. His cartoons attacked political corruption and public ignorance.

suspension bridge, a roadway suspended from wire ropes. Ottmar Mergenthaler invented a machine that a printer could use to set a line of type in seconds. Before his invention, each letter had to be set by hand, and the process of setting type to print a page took hours.

Preservation of the German language was one of the keys to maintaining cultural traditions that united the communities. Not only were church services in German, so were classes in the public schools of Cincinnati, Milwaukee, and St. Louis.

Thomas Nast, born in Germany in 1840, was destined to become the most important political cartoonist in the 19th century. Nast trained

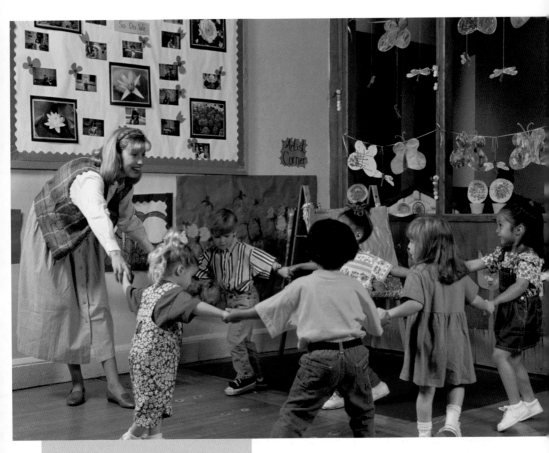

German immigrants introduced the idea of kindergarten (in German, "children's garden") to the United States in the 1850s.

his artist's brush on a polititian named William M. "Boss" Tweed, whose corrupt Tammany Hall organization dominated New York City government and stole millions of dollars from taxpayers. He also created the popular images of Santa Claus, the Democratic donkey, and the Republican elephant.

Education was heavily emphasized in German American families. Margaretha Meyer Schurz started the first kindergarten in the U.S. to prepare children for regular schooling. Gymnasiums and physical education programs, found in virtually every high school today, reflect the influences of the German-American Turners who started such programs of physical fitness in the 19th century.

German traditions are deeply embedded in the culture of the U.S., so much so that many people are unaware of their origins. The Christmas tree began as a German custom in pre-Christian times. It first appeared in America in Lancaster, Pennsylvania, in 1821. An evergreen tree, still colorful in winter, was a reminder that spring would one day come. Germans decorated their trees with candy, fruit, and gingerbread.

Easter is another holiday influenced by German culture. Coloring

GERMAN-AMERICAN LANGUAGE IN NORTH AMERICA

Henry Louis Mencken (1880-1956) was a journalist, editor, and literary critic in Baltimore whose study of language, *The American Language,* has become a classic in investigating the origins of distinctly American words. Mencken, a German-American himself, took a considerable interest in the German-American cultural heritage. He was one of the first to discover that many German words have found their way into American vocabulary.

Some of the following words are German in origin, but are now so common in American English that they are considered part of the American language: beer garden, stein, spritz, gestalt, angst, flak, concertmaster, waltz, yodel, zigzag, kaput, wanderlust, iceberg, kindergarten, Kris Kringle, paraffin, plunder, and cookbook.

Albert Einstein is perhaps one of the most famous thinkers of the modern era. He developed the revolutionary theory of relativity and was awarded the Nobel Prize in 1921. Einstein became a U.S. citizen in 1940.

of eggs began in the Middle Ages as a special treat at Easter because Christians were not allowed to eat eggs during the religious season of Lent. The hare, or rabbit, became a symbol of Easter because the Christian holiday of Easter is celebrated on the Sunday after the first full moon of spring. Pennsylvanian children built nests in the fields for the Easter hare, believing that if they were good the hare would lay eggs in the nest. On Easter, the children went into their fields with baskets to collect the eggs, which had been set out by their parents.

German music served to unite both the old country and the new. Notable German-American composers and musicians include Paul

Hindemuth, Oscar Hammerstein, Hans Zimmer, Franz Waxman, Walter Damrosch, and Kurt Weill. Painters such as Albert Bierstadt, architects Walter Gropious and Ludwig Mies van der Rohe, photographer Albert Eisenstadt, and movie director Woody Allen all have German ancestry.

Scientists such as the great Albert Einstein were refugees who relocated to America and helped forge our scientific heritage. J. Robert Oppenheimer and Wernher von Braun, who helped develop America's space program, were scientists who created a partnership between government and science in the nuclear age. Oppenheimer, a theoretical physicist, played a key role in helping the United States to develop the atomic bomb during World War II. Braun, a German rocket scientist, was an instrumental part of America's space program during the 1950s and 1960s. Rockets developed under Braun's leadership helped American astronauts reach the moon in July 1969.

Today, the highest percentage of German Americans live in Wisconsin, followed by North and South Dakota, Nebraska, Iowa, and Minnesota. In the 2006 American Community Survey, 17 percent of Americans claimed to be of German ancestry.

Famous German Americans

ARTISTS AND ARCHITECTS
John A. Roebling, civil engineer and bridge builder
Ludwig Mies van der Rohe, architect
Albert Bierstadt, landscape painter
Alfred Eisenstaedt, photographer
Emanuel Leutze, painter
Thomas Nast, political cartoonist
Charles M. Schulz, Peanuts cartoonist
Alfred Stieglitz, artistic photographer

BUSINESS OWNERS/ENTREPRENEURS
Andy Bechtolsheim, co-founder of Sun Microsystems
William Edward Boeing, founder of aircraft manufacturer Boeing.
Adolphus Busch, brewer
Walter Chrysler, automobile developer
Walt Disney, pioneering film producer
Henry J. Heinz, ketchup company founder
Milton S. Hershey, chocolate company founder
Conrad Hilton, hotel chain founder
Oscar Mayer, meat company founder
William Rittenhouse, built the first paper mill in America
John D. Rockefeller, industrialist
Eric E. Schmidt, chairman and CEO of Google
Levi Strauss, blue jeans maker
George Westinghouse, engineer and electricity pioneer

ENTERTAINERS
Woody Allen, film director
Fred Astaire, dancer and actor
Johnny Depp, actor
Douglas Fairbanks, actor of the silent era
Harrison Ford, actor.
Clark Gable, actor
Wolfgang Petersen, film director
Johnny Weissmuller, actor and Olympic swimmer
Bruce Willis, actor
Darryl F. Zanuck, early Hollywood producer

JOURNALISTS/AUTHORS
H. L. Mencken, social critic
L. Frank Baum , Wizard of Oz creator
Theodore Dreiser, author

H. L. Mencken, muckraking journalist
Sylvia Plath, poet
Gertrude Stein, writer
John Steinbeck, Nobel Prize-winning author
Dr. Seuss (Theodor Seuss Geisel), children's writer and illustrator
Kurt Vonnegut, novelist

MUSICIANS

Walter J. Damrosch, conductor
Fred Durst, Limp Bizkit founder
Paul Hindemith, composer and violinist
Dave Grohl, rock musician and songwriter
Jeff Schroeder, Smashing Pumpkins guitarist

POLITICAL AND HISTORICAL FIGURES

Neil Armstrong, first man on the Moon
Warren E. Burger, Supreme Court chief justice
Dwight D. Eisenhower, U.S. president
Herbert Hoover, U.S. president
Henry Kissinger, statesman
Chester W. Nimitz, World War II admiral
Franz Daniel Pastorius, founder of Germantown, Pennsylvania
John J. Pershing, World War I commanding general
Walter Reuther, labor leader
Theodore Roosevelt, U.S. president
Carl Schurz, politician
Norman Schwarzkopf Jr., commander during 1991 Gulf War
Margarethe Meyer Schurz, established the kindergarten system

SCIENTISTS

Albert Einstein, theoretical physicist
Maria Goeppert-Mayer, Nobel Prize-winning physicist
J. Robert Oppenheimer, "Father of the Atomic Bomb"
Wernher von Braun, rocket builder

SPORTS

Dale Earnhardt, NASCAR driver
Gertrude Ederle, first woman to swim the English Channel
Jack Nicklaus, professional golfer
Babe Ruth, baseball player
Brian Urlacher, Pro Bowl linebacker
Wes Welker, NFL wide receiver

Glossary

Accommodations lodging, food, and services.

Agnostic not committed to believing in the existence or nonexistence of God.

Anti-Semitism hostility toward or discrimination against Jews as a religious, ethnic, or racial group.

Apprentice one who is learning a trade or art by practicing under skilled workers.

Artisan someone who specializes in a craft or trade.

Assimilation the absorption of a culture or group into a larger body.

Berth a place to sit or sleep on a ship.

Cobbler a person who makes and mends shoes and other leather goods.

Congregation a group of people who meet for worship and religious instruction.

Emigrant someone who leaves his or her native country to start a new life in a new country.

Ethnicity an affiliation or quality of a particular ethnic group.

Guild a medieval association of artists and craftsmen.

Hardtack a cracker-like biscuit made of flour, salt, and water.

Hessian a German mercenary serving in the British forces during the American Revolution.

Indentured servant a person who is bound by an agreement to work for another for a specified time, usually in return for payment of travel and living expenses.

Masonry the act of making bricks.

Peasant apoor agricultural worker in Europe, or member of the lowest class.

Persecution the act of harassing someone because of his or her beliefs.

Sweatshop a workplace that is often overcrowded and unhealthy where workers often earn low wages.

Trachoma a contagious bacterial eye disease.

Visa a stamp on a passport indicating that a person has permission to enter a country.

Further Reading

Cieslik, Thomas, et al, editors. *Immigration: A Documentary and Reference Guide*. Westport, Conn.: Greenhaven Press, 2008.

Hoobler, Thomas and Dorothy Hoobler. *German American Family Album*. New York: Oxford University Press, 1996.

Katz, William Loren. *A History of Multicultural America: the Great Migrations 1800s–1912*. Austin: Raintree Steck-Vaughn Publishers, 1996.

Magocss, Paul R. *The Encyclopedia of Canada's Peoples*. Toronto, Canada. 1998.

O'Donnell. *U.S. Immigration*. Mankato, Minn.: Capstone Press, 2008.

Skal, George von. *History of German Immigration in the United States*. Whitefish, MT: Kessinger Publishing, 2008.

Trumbauer, Lisa. *German Immigration*. New York: Facts on File, 2004.

Tracing Your German-American Ancestors

Carmack, Sharon DeBartolo. *A Genealogist's Guide to Discovering Your Immigrant and Ethnic Ancestors*. Cincinnati: Betterway Books, 2000.

Jones, George F. *German-American Names*. 2nd ed. Baltimore: genealogical Publishing Co., 1995.

Tolzmann, Don Heinrich, ed. *German Immigration to America: The First Wave*. Bowie, Md.: Heritage Books, 1993.

Internet Resources

http://www.census.gov

The official Web site of the U.S. Bureau of the Census contains information about the most recent census taken in 2000.

http://www12.statcan.ca/english/census/index.cfm

The Web site for Canada's Bureau of Statistics, which includes population information updated for the most recent census in May 2006.

http://www.pgs.org/

The official Web site for the Pennsylvania German Society, a non-profit organization dedicated to the preservation of the 300-year history of Pennsylvania's German Americans.

http://www.gahfusa.org/

The Web site for the only national umbrella organization representing Americans of German ancestry.

http://www.ellisisland.org/

This Web site is devoted to the history of Ellis Island and the immigrants who came through its doors.

http://www.dank.org/

The Web site for the largest organization of German Americans. The organization seeks to preserve the ancestry and culture of Americans of German descent.

Publisher's Note: The Web sites listed on this page were active at the time of publication. The publisher is not responsible for Web sites that have changed their address or discontinued operation since the date of publication. The publisher reviews and updates the websites each time the book is reprinted.

Index

Photo Credits

Page

2: David & Peter Turnley/Corbis
10: Bettmann/Corbis
13: Hulton/Archive
14: Adam Woolfitt/Corbis
18: Hulton/Archive
20: Corbis Images
22: Photos.com
23: used under license from
    Shutterstock, Inc.
24: Independence National Historical
    Park, Philadelphia
27: used under license from
    Shutterstock, Inc.
29: used under license from
    Shutterstock, Inc.
30: Library of Congress
32: used under license from
    Shutterstock, Inc.

35: Bettmann/Corbis
36: Bettmann/Corbis
39: both Corbis Images
40: Hulton/Archive
43: Hulton/Archive
44: Bettmann/Corbis
47: used under license from
    Shutterstock, Inc.
48: used under license from
    Shutterstock, Inc.;
    (inset) Library of Congress
50: Library of Congress
51: Library of Congress
52: Photos.com
54: Bettmann/Corbis

Contributors

Barry Moreno has been librarian and historian at the Ellis Island Immigration Museum and the Statue of Liberty National Monument since 1988. He is the author of *The Statue of Liberty Encyclopedia*, which was published by Simon & Schuster in October 2000. He is a native of Los Angeles, California. After graduation from California State University at Los Angeles, where he earned a degree in history, he joined the National Park Service as a seasonal park ranger at the Statue of Liberty; he eventually became the monument's librarian. In his spare time, Barry enjoys reading, writing, and studying foreign languages and grammar. His biography has been included in *Who's Who Among Hispanic Americans*, *The Directory of National Park Service Historians*, *Who's Who in America*, and *The Directory of American Scholars*.

A writer of German and Irish descent, **Peg Ashbrock** has been writing her whole career, first in television journalism and now in books and magazines. She lives with her family in Cincinnati, Ohio. When she is not writing, Peg spends her days traveling with her husband, David, or carpooling and cheering her three children, Tori, Meghan, and Jon.